AND DON'T TELL ANYONE

And Don't Tell Anyone

Healing from Incest Through Poetry and Art

by

Abigail Brown

NORTH STAR PRESS OF ST. CLOUD, INC.

Special thanks to Kara K. Bichler for her editorial assistance.

Printed in the United States of America by
Park Press Quality Printing, Inc., Waite Park, Minnesota.

Published by
North Star Press of St. Cloud, Inc.
P.O. Box 451
St. Cloud, Minnesota 56302

International Standard Book Number: 0-87839-109-6

1 2 3 4 5 6 7 8 9 10

The truth
painful, infrequently
profitable, usually
disturbing
a positive value
in order not to offend
Should I think better of the telling?

Should I keep the truth imprisoned?
The maggot in my brain?
Cut and run?
to remove the sting
and the crudeness
of a father's gutter language
and a father's gutter actions
What parts must I leave out
so that you and I do not redden
with the telling?

And Don't Tell Anyone
is not safe
is not polite
is not sterile
It tells all
and it hides nothing

The truth of remembrance
shines on the beautiful
shines on the ugly
it relieves anguish
it relieves joy
and it asks for meaning

Women
have been trained
to be nice
and to hide our anger
and our fury
As we hide behind
petticoats and aprons
and downcast eyes

AND DON'T TELL ANYONE

We must "bruise the perpetrators
with a rod of iron
and break them in pieces
like a potter's vessel
Our wrath be kindled
Only then may women lay down in peace
and rest and dwell in safety"

Psalter—Book of Common Prayer
Psalter of David; excerpts from Psalms 2-4

I am seventy years old
mother of five
and grandmother of thirteen
I was born
before Lindbergh flew the ocean
before days of commercial air travel
before ball point pens
and plastic
Before television, Guess jeans and Nikes

On the day I was born,
two Negro youths were lynched
In Fort Myers,
some things change
and others do not
That is why
I tell this story
because the world
hasn't changed
all that much
these seventy years

My story
and so many like it
lives on
in the flesh of sisters
Twenty years ago
I could not and would not
breathe the word—incest
I would hide behind
lacy veils of front parlor curtains

But now,
I share this telling
With prayers for change
for an end to violence
against women and children
The old ways
are gagging us
They allow the old secrets
to sneak on
to conceal
to hush over
the whispers lurking in the shadows
and mask
of the night
that keeps all women
trapped
unable to break free
of the cords that bind us

Buried shame
desperation
frenzy
Black bile memories
remembered deep
inside my body
My father's iron fist
controlling from the crypt
all my long, long years
all my seventy years

In the house
of the dead
all does not die
But snakes out
of the grave
hissing
poisoning
writhing
squeezing
encircling
A shrouded soul
forever imprisoned
by a grave ghoul

Run through
with the old hauntings
disabled
gasping
struggling to breathe
struggling to get a life
To brand the memory
It must hurt
To hurt is to heal
To heal is to sacrifice
Trained to sacrifice
black bile memories
I have shared with you

These seventy years
as I trudged long, long, long
Dirging a song, song, song
The lane I went was long, long, long
and the verse I sang
was black rot memory
of my father's usage
of my body

Don't talk about it
Don't think about it
Don't deal with it

I hammer at fury in my body
I drum at anguish in my body
I pound at shame in my body
I beat at loathing in my body
I scream at the black rot memories

Demons of gangrene rot in my body
tomorrow and tomorrow
My father
still thrusting
still controlling
still possessing
my body

Sing a song of sixpence
pocket full of rye
Four and twenty blackbirds
baked in a pie
and when the pie was opened,
the birds began to sing
Now, wasn't that a dainty dish
Sing, sing, what shall I sing?
Sing a song of incest
incest words are vulgar
incest is vulgar
My daddy's language was vulgar
what he did
and the words of his mouth
are Siamese twinned
forever
in my mind
I cannot split apart
the one from the other
My daddy's song
not a dainty dish

In the sequence of the birthing
of this book,
It was first painted
saying the unmentionable
with color and brush
The world seldom pauses
To decipher paint
but the world does notice words
To write was frightening
horrific
The topic of this book
is a common experience
An experience of mine
An experience of many
It should not be the experience
of anyone

Jane be nimble
Jane be quick
Jane jumped over the lilac hedge
by the alley
where daddy hides the Old Grand Dad
or in the culvert
by St. Luke's Church
or under the woodpile
in the cellar

Daddy is home
all boozed up
and mama gets pissed
and yells at daddy
he flies off the handle
and takes after mama

Mama's voice boils
"And where is the money now
for the Piggly Wiggly bill
and the stove kerosene
and the Maytag payment?"
Daddy's fists fly
exploding on mama
and she stumbles, bawling
banging the porch door
and runs down the alley
past the parish hall
past the yellow rose hedge
I am scared for mama
I am scared for me

Alone now with daddy
alone in my bedroom
shivering and hiding
under Granny Emma's pink wedding ring quilt
cringing from the monster shadow
that devours my bed and
jerks off the quilt and
pokes at my shaking

Darkness descends and I space out
"You never say no to daddy"
Nor to Tom
Dick
or Harry
I learned it well
It pissed me off

Shim, sham shimmy
shame on you
I hold shame
in my body
I am two sets of dishes
that do not match

Flow over my broken patterns
made of porcelain,
pure and white
without blemish
So that I match
so that I go together
so that I am complete

I will have
no shame

Cover over the secrets
of the night
and kill my soul maggots

My exhausted mama
pushed out birth heads yearly
and then turned her face
and closed her mind,
her eyes
her bedroom door,
and slept alone

Years later
a boyfriend spit it out
"If I'd known your daddy
was messing around with you
I'd never given you the time of day"

My mind
my body
muddied with shame.
Shim, sham, shimmy,
shame on you

Stop my heart!
Smother my breath!
I would be a dust speck
I would be a mouse
I would be a spider
and crawl under the bed
Away
away in a corner
away from Daddy's shadow
away from sour beer breath
and fetid penis
swollen huge

"There was a crooked man
he ran a crooked mile"

I dreamed of an evil man
he ran an evil mile
Chasing his daughter
across an evil stile

Run, run as fast as you can
You can't run from me
I'm not the gingerbread man
I'm the fox man

The frenzy of my dream
flashes, pulsates
buzzes, thick as bees
in my head
round and round
as the tidal roar splashes
crashing onto rocks and reefs
grinding gravel to sand
round and round
down and down

Nighmare shrieks
split my throat
"Daddy wants a bedtime treat"
Where to go?
Where to run?
away from the dream phantom
convulsing
whirling
tumbling me
into the black of night hauntings

Run, run as fast as you can
Raw breath
slices
shatters
and daddy's shadow racing up fast behind me
"Jack it off, Baby,
Daddy wants a joy ride"
No place to hide—
(not under the bridge
and not up the tree)
from fox man
Tongue hanging out
eyes glittering
joy stick hard between his legs
Run, run as fast as you can

You shall have an apple
You shall have a plum
You shall have a belting
when your daddy comes home
"Dance to your daddy, my lassie
and be on that bed
belly side down
with your pants off
and your ass bare
on Tuesday night
at seven"

And this day only Friday
four days
and four nights
till nightmare of daddy's belting
for coming home late
from the library next door

Terror of belt
stripped from daddy's pants
whacking!
burning!
"Hurts me worse than it does you"
Daddy gasps
jollied with beer
and welts and blood
he gets it on

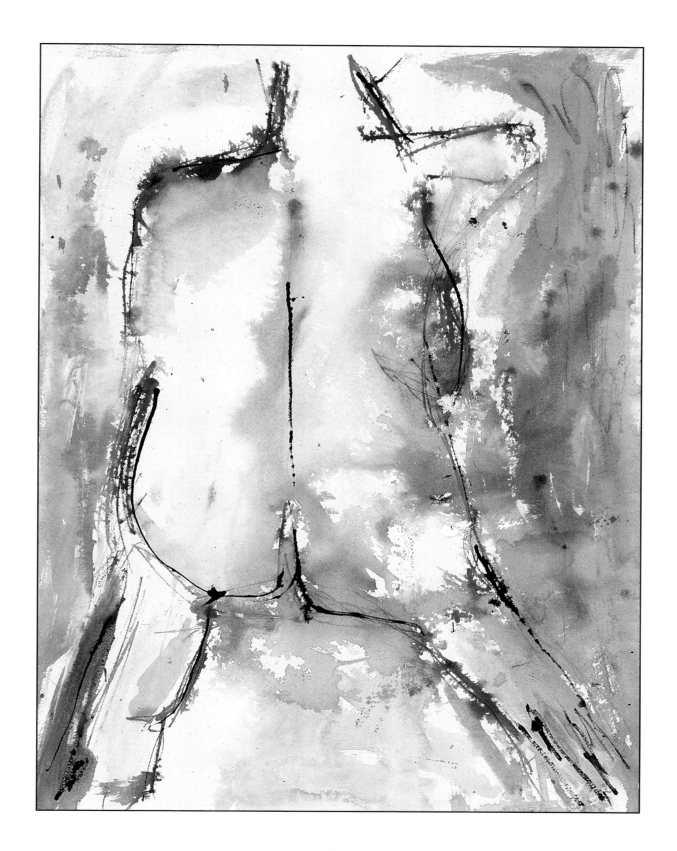

Harpies of pain
clench my belly
The curse
menstrual vampire devils
doubles me over
victim of my body
my loathsome body
A lewd lightning rod
red is a petticoat, all taffeta
is a Coty lipstick
is cunt blood
and red rags

Soaking in a pail of cold water
alms and oblations
at the altar of the Father
oblation of blood
oblation of pain
loot of the patriarch
the father claims his entitlement

Hiding the deepest, silent
darkness of the night
Years of physical abuse
and sexual subjugation
Took my life away
Emotional and mental castration
A nothing
What I would or wish was nothing

Dragging the shame of my father's sins
inside me
like a cancer
it grows
mortifies
gnaws
corrodes
sickens
But I would tell nothing
not speak of it to anyone
If no one else knows
the secrets of the night
then I am a regular person
like you

Frozen screams
Choke my throat.
Daddy's got a hard-on.
"Take that prick
Into your mouth, Kid."
Down your throat.
Hot sperm dump!
"And no back talk to your dad."
God is male;
The male is god.
Submit!
Submit!
Wives to the god/husband
Daughter to the god/father.
"Daddy loves you, baby.
Oh, ain't it fun!
Sweet baby that sucks off
her daddy."
Suck it off for Jesus.
"And we won't tell mama,
Or belt you good.
Belt you dead."

A nursery rhyme I hated
Taught to me by daddy

Here I sit
a pretty little figure
If the boys
don't like me now
They will
when I grow bigger

Stand on the chair
recite it for your daddy
Say it! Say it!
Daddy's pretty package

Ugly rhyme
Ugly body

"Donkey, donkey, old and gray,
Open your mouth and loudly bray;
Lift your ears and blow your horns,
To wake the world this sleepy morn'."

Roses are red
Violets are blue
My daddy's not sweet

And I am red with rage
Scarlet frenzy engulfs my body
fierce dragons
inflame my being

The rage
and the haunting
and the pain
my body struggles to contain
erupts into a flash fire
Blazing out of control
explodes
scorches
fiery volcanic eruptions
scalds my insides
and leave me cindered

Rage flares out
and smashes relationships
makes me explode
makes me roar
Who am I?
what are my boundaries?
And what are your boundaries?
Do I have any?
And why can't I say,
"No, I'd rather not,"

A missed childhood
and grief for the little girl
who never was
No innocence
(at age three
stood on a chair
placed there by daddy,
the better to suck cock)
Outraged
that I never had a chance
to choose a sexual partner
all my life
Always chosen
by the man

44

"When God hands you a gift,
he also hands you a whip
and the whip is intended
for self-flagellation only"

Truman Capote

As the potter throws, shapes clay
and fires the mud
As the iron monger
shapes molten ore
into a vessel
My childhood
formed the vessel
I have become
The fired clay
the melting iron
are all past tense
but the shape taken
stays with me still

Each day,
the mold must be smashed
over and over again

My father planted his garden
in rows
north to south
I plant my garden
east to west
breaking the pattern

"Ding dong bell
pussy's in the well"
Daddy put her in
who pulled her out?
The magic
of a paintbrush
pulled her out

My own canvas
My own brush
My own choices
My own images
erupting from my soul
through a sacramental paintbrush
When I was middle aged
I began to follow
"the devices and desires of my own heart"
I was no longer
"a paper doll to call his own"
released from the Medusa snakes
that turn the soul to stone

48

I let go!
I dance!
I am alive!
I possess myself!
I sing my own melody!
I dance my own movements!
I write my own words!
I paint my own colors!
I play my own rhythms!
I express it!
I choose it!
I give birth!

No longer the child of stone
mute
ashamed
alone
No longer dwelling
in the cave of my soul
But one who found her voice
in a paint brush
each painting a new birth
another soul layer
breaking out of the old

Free at last
free from the lies of childhood
free from the bedtime stories
I paint it out
I sing
I shout
Praise the almighty
free at last

"For every evil under the sun
there is a remedy or there is none
If there is one, seek till you find it
if there be none, never mind it"
Sisters, seek till you find it

"And when the pie was opened
the birds began to sing"

We will remember
we will not forget
we must tell what happened
we must understand what happened
we must grow and
we must celebrate

And Don't Tell Anyone was painted and written in spite of, not because of myself.
The painting leapt out of a possessed paintbrush with an energy level so high,
it left me feverish. The brush was alive with a will of its own. I truly
believe the book was guided by the spirit of my deceased father channeling
and cleansing his immortal soul on another level of existence.
A healing for him. A healing for me.